CRABTREE
www.crabtreebooks.com

NATURE UNFOLDS
THE TROPICAL RAINFOREST

SWAMPLANDS

CONTENTS

CAPUCHIN MONKEY ►

Capuchins are heavier than squirrel monkeys, but they are still light enough to move among the branches of the upper canopy. They eat fruit, nuts, and leaves. Capuchins also hunt for insects and small animals such as birds and lizards. Sometimes they move to lower levels to play and search for food.

◄ Capuchin monkeys raid birds' nests for eggs.

► OROPENDOLA

It can be difficult finding a nesting place that is safe from enemies. The oropendola solves this problem by building a hanging nest. It uses its beak to weave together pieces of plants such as grass stems and strips of leaves. The woven nest is very strong. Since it hangs, it is difficult for most predators to reach. The female builds the nest while the male performs a mating **display**.

► MORPHO BUTTERFLY

Male morphos have vivid blue wings, which helps them attract females. Females are dull brown. Females pick the largest and bluest male to be their mate.

◄ BLACK-THROATED TROGON

Trogons are well suited to clinging to tree trunks. Two of the four toes on each foot point backward, which allows the bird to grip bark. Stiff tail feathers help support the bird while it clings to the trunk and pecks in search of small insects.

► Macaws live in very cramped quarters.

HARPY EAGLE ►

The harpy eagle is the largest bird in the rainforest. It has fairly short wings for darting between branches after prey such as monkeys, sloths, and other small mammals.

MACAWS ►

These colorful long-tailed parrots often nibble on soft rocks. Their food does not contain all of the **nutrients** they need, and the rocks provide important minerals. Their nests are made in small tree hollows. The parents have to clamber over their chicks to feed them. Things get very cramped by the time the chicks are ready to leave the nest.

◄ A chick begins to resemble its parents when its feathers grow in.

Rainforest

LOWER CANOPY

This layer is the busiest one in the tropical forest. The branches here are thicker than in the upper canopy, so they can hold larger, heavier animals.

Since the upper canopy blocks a lot of the sunlight, the lower canopy is much darker. The animals cannot always see well in the dim light. Most animals rely on other senses to find their way around, locate food, and avoid danger.

◄ ORCHID BEE
Orchid bees pollinate orchids as they collect pollen and nectar to eat.

HOWLER MONKEYS ►

Large monkeys such as the howlers are too heavy to climb above the branches of the lower canopy. They often lose sight of each other in the dim lower canopy, so they rely on their voices to communicate. Their loud, booming howl is created by forcing air through their extra-large voice box.

► The air-sac in the howler's throat inflates to force air through the voice box, or larynx.

GREEN-CHEEKED HUMMINGBIRD ►

Hummingbirds are the smallest birds. They are so tiny that they can build their nests on the thinnest twigs and leaves. They are able to hover like helicopters, which allows them to hang in the air and suck nectar from dangling flowers.

► Birds and lizards often check bromeliads for the prey shown here.

TOUCANS ►

Most people can recognize toucans by their large, colorful beaks. The birds use their beaks to signal to each other across the forest canopy. Their long, lightweight bill also allows toucans to reach and pick fruits off branches that are too thin to support their body weight.

Toucans toss fruit into the air to pass it from their beak to their throat. ►

◄ QUETZAL
While hovering under the branches, this rare bird feeds by grabbing insects and fruit from trees.

◄ An ancient Olmec carving of a quetzal.

SPIDER MONKEYS ►

Spider monkeys have a **prehensile tail**, which means they can use it to grab branches as if it were an extra arm. It has a leathery pad that provides better grip. These lightweight monkeys can reach most fruits by hanging from their tail. They also use their tails to escape predators by swinging quickly from branch to branch. ►

► The pad is on the underside of the tail.

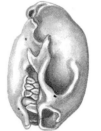

▲ EMERALD TREE BOA

The emerald tree boa is well camouflaged among leafy branches, and it can strike quickly to surprise its prey. Boas kill their prey by squeezing it until it can no longer breathe. They swallow prey whole, and a single meal may last them several days.

A woodpecker drilling holes ▶

▼ WOODPECKER

The woodpecker feeds mainly on grubs. It taps bark with its beak to feel and listen for the hollows grubs live in. When it finds a grub, it hammers a hole with its beak and grabs the prey. Woodpeckers have special skulls that absorb the shock of hammering.

▶ The woodpecker coils its long tongue inside its skull when not using it.

BRAZIL NUT ▶

These nuts are similar in shape to an orange segment and grow inside a large, round fruit. When the fruit falls from a branch, it hits other branches on its way to the forest floor. It bursts and scatters the nuts, which are large seeds.

▼ RHINOCEROS BEETLE

Adult males have a growth like a rhinoceros horn, which is how they got their name. They use the horn to fight with other males. The winner gets to mate with the female of his choice. These beetles can be up to five inches (13 cm) long.

BROMELIADS ▲

These plants are **epiphytes**. They grow on the branches of trees but do not harm them. Their harging roots collect water from the air. Bromeliads also collect rainwater in their funnel-shaped leaves. The pools of water in their leaves provide a home to various small animals, such as tree frogs, snails, and leeches.

GECKO ▲
Geckos have special feet that can grip even the most slippery leaves.

▶ TWO-TOED SLOTH

Two-toed sloths are smaller and more active than their cousin, the three-toed sloth. Sloths are the slowest moving land animals. Since they cannot outrun enemies, sloths avoid being eaten by gripping branches so tightly that they cannot be pulled down.

▲ The sloth skull shows the cheek teeth, which the animal uses to chew its food.

▲ Each front limb has two toes.

▶ Brazil nut

MOUSE OPOSSUM

Opossums are the only group of **marsupials** found outside of Australia. Baby marsupials are tiny when they are born. They move to a pouch on their mother's body, where they keep growing. When they are big enough to leave the pouch, they ride on their mother's back. ▶

▲ CATTLEYA ORCHID
This orchid is an epiphyte.

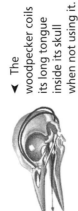

LEAF-CUTTER ANT

These ants have scissor-like jaws for cutting leaves. They carry the pieces to their nests and leave them to grow mold, which they eat.

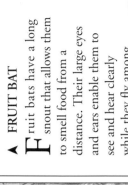

TREE PORCUPINE

This porcupine has shorter quills than ground-living ones because it must be able to climb between branches easily. To rest, the porcupine wraps its tail around a branch and hangs upside-down. It feeds mainly on leaves. ▶

◀ SPECTACLED OWL

The spectacled owl is an excellent nocturnal hunter. With sharp eyesight and silent wings, it swoops down and snatches animals by surprise.

◀ FRUIT BAT

Fruit bats have a long snout that allows them to smell food from a distance. Their large eyes and ears enable them to see and hear clearly while they fly among the trees at night.

Rainforest
UNDERSTORY

The understory is a dark place. Few animals spend all their time here. It is crisscrossed mainly by animals on their way to the canopy or the forest floor. Some birds and mammals nest and raise their young in the smaller trees, where they can hide from many of the large hunting birds that fly above the canopy. Many other predators hunt in the understory so the young must be guarded closely.

RUBY TOPAZ HUMMINGBIRD ▶

Hummingbirds flap their wings so quickly that they appear to be a blur. The wings move back and forth, holding the bird still while it feeds on the nectar of a flower.

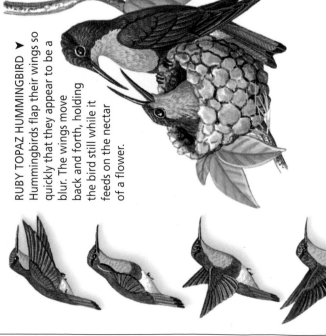

◀ These pictures show how its wings move when a hummingbird hovers.

▶ THREE-TOED SLOTH

This sloth has a type of algae growing on its fur. The algae turn from green to brown at different times of the year and help camouflage the sloth. Sloths have such weak legs that they cannot walk. They hang from branches and rarely go down to the ground.

Moths feed on the algae that grow on sloths. ▶

Douroucouli eyes are large and reflective to see well in the dark of night. ▶

DOUROUCOULI ▲

This nocturnal monkey is also called the "night monkey." Like most nocturnal animals, douroucoulis have large eyes to gather as much light as possible. Their diet consists of fruit, leaves, and insects.

CANNONBALL FRUITS AND FLOWERS ▶

The tropical rainforest does not go through seasons as forests in other areas do, so its trees can produce flowers, seeds, and fruit at the same time.

▼ OCELOT

This wild cat hunts smaller animals such as birds, monkeys, and this agouti. Its spotted coat helps camouflage the ocelot by mimicking the dappled pattern of sunlight breaking through the canopy above. Ocelots are hunted by humans for their highly valued skins.

▲ POISON ARROW FROGS

These frogs come in a range of patterns and bright colors. The colors warn predators that they are poisonous. Their poison is so powerful that it is used by forest peoples for hunting. They apply it to their arrow heads. When an animal is hit with one of these arrows, it dies very quickly.

▲ People roast the frogs over a fire, which causes the poison to ooze out. They then rub their arrow-tips across the frog's skin.

▶ TAMANDUA

The tamandua is a **nocturnal** anteater that spends most of its time asleep in the trees. It uses its sharp claws to rip open rotten stumps and branches in search of its favorite food—ants. It also eats termites and grubs. When threatened, the tamandua rears up on its hind legs and slashes and hisses at the predator.

▲ The tamandua's heavy-duty claws make good weapons.

RING-TAILED COATI ▶

Coatis forage in groups, searching for plants, fruit, lizards, and mice. The food is shared among the group. Staying in groups helps protect them from enemies. They hold their long, striped tails upright so that each coati can see at a glance where the others are in times of danger.

◀ BROCKET DEER
This deer is well suited to the dense forest. It is small enough to slip easily between shrubs and other plants. Its antlers point backward, so they do not snag on branches when it runs from enemies.

JAGUAR ▶
These big cats are usually tan with darker spots, but sometimes they are black. Jaguars like the water and are usually found near streams or rivers. They are active at night, when they hunt large land animals such as deer, capybaras, and tapirs. Jaguars quietly creep up on their prey and then leap on it by surprise. They bite the animal's neck with their powerful jaws. Jaguars also hunt other prey, such as fish. They sit patiently on fallen logs and snatch the fish out of the water with their sharp claws.

Rainforest

FOREST FLOOR

When fruits, leaves, branches, and even dead animals fall from the higher layers of the rainforest, they usually end up on the forest floor. Fungi, bacteria, and **invertebrates** feed on and break down the decaying plants and animals. They help create a thin layer of fertile soil called **humus**. Besides small, ground-living animals, the largest animals of the Amazon are also found on the forest floor.

Tayras often raid nests to snatch eggs or chicks. ▶

◀ TAYRA
The tayra is related to weasels, otters, badgers, and skunks. Tayras are good swimmers and climbers. They eat a wide variety of foods, including fruit and small animals such as squirrels and birds. In turn, they are hunted by jaguars. Tayras are often found in pairs or family groups.

▶ The tayra is a good hunter on the ground and in the trees.

▶ Its front claws are so big that an anteater must walk on its knuckles.

BOA CONSTRICTOR

Boa constrictors ambush their prey. They quickly coil around the surprised animal and squeeze, or constrict, it so that it cannot breathe. When the animal dies, the snake dislocates, or unhinges, its jaws and swallows its prey headfirst.

ARMADILLO ▶

Armadillos are protected from the teeth and claws of predators by bony plates of armor. They have powerful claws on their front feet, which they use to dig for insects. They are active mainly at night, when they also hunt for small reptiles and amphibians.

▶ The tapir's snout is soft and flexible.

TAPIR

Tapirs have a sensitive snout, which they use to sniff out fallen fruits and nuts on the forest floor. Baby tapirs have a pattern of stripes and spots that helps camouflage them on the dappled ground. ▶

◀ BASILISK LIZARD

This unusual lizard can walk on water. It moves so quickly over the surface that its feet touch the water for only a split-second, so it does not have time to sink. The basilisk dashes across water only when it is in danger.

GIANT ANTEATER ▶

Giant anteaters have very strong front legs with huge claws. They use them to rip open termite and ant nests. They use their long, sticky tongue to lap up thousands of the insects. Anteaters have a tube-shaped mouth with no teeth. Baby anteaters ride on their mother's back until they are big enough to fend for themselves.

◀ Anteater skull

▲ An anteater can flick its tongue more than 100 times a minute when feeding.

◀ COLLARED PECCARY

Peccaries are wild hogs. They forage in large herds and can be dangerous. Other animals often flee from peccary herds because peccaries will attack from all sides. They eat almost anything.

◀ A peccary has sharp teeth to rip flesh and flat ones to grind plants.

TRUMPETER BIRD ▶

These birds are named for their trumpet-like call. They work together to hunt snakes. One bird pecks the snake's head while the others hold it.

White-Collared
Swifts (4)

Rainforest

KEY TO FOLD-OUT

Use these key numbers if you
want to identify any of the
animals and plants on the
Rainforest fold-out. Most of
them are featured on pages
28-35, and they are listed here
in bold type. Animals that are
not featured are keyed, listed,
and described here.

Quetzal (22)

1 Swallow-Tailed Kite
2 Yellow-Chevroned Parakeet
  Parakeets are small parrots with
  long tails. They eat fruit, seeds,
  and nuts.
3 Harpy Eagle
4 White-Collared Swift
5 Black-Throated Trogon
6 Tanager
  Tanagers eat fruit, seeds, and a
  few insects. Some species are
  among the most colorful birds in
  the world.
7 Yellow Conure (see page 15)
8 Red-Ruffed Fruit Crow
9 King Vulture
10 Oropendola
11 Squirrel Monkey

39 Tamarin
   Tamarins are miniature monkeys. They
   feed on fruit, eggs, and insects.
40 **Ruby Topaz Hummingbird**
41 **Passion Flower**
   The passion flower is a climbing vine.
   Its flowers are waxy and tough enough
   to survive the beaks of hummingbirds.
42 Guan
   These birds of the forest floor are
   drawn to fire. Native peoples hunt
   them by using flaming torches as lures.
43 **Cannonball Fruits and Flowers**
44 **Ocelot**
45 **Spectacled Owl**
46 **Three-Toed Sloth**
47 **Douroucouli**
48 Rufous Jacamar
   Jacamars are similar to
   hummingbirds, but they eat
   insects instead of nectar.
49 Ithomiid Butterfly
   There are many species of
   these colorful butterflies
   in the Amazon rainforest.
   They gather in groups to
   feed on forest flowers.
50 **Tamandua**
51 **Leaf-Cutter Ant**
52 **Brocket Deer**
53 **Ring-Tailed Coati**
54 Tayra
55 **Trumpeter Bird**
56 **Collared Peccary**
57 **Giant Anteater**
58 **Boa Constrictor**
59 Armadillo
60 **Tapir**
61 **Jaguar**
62 Lobster Claw
   The clusters of this plant are designed
   to attract pollinating animals.

Woodpecker (21)

The clusters of this plant are designed
to attract pollinating animals.

NATURE UNFOLDS

THE TROPICAL RAINFOREST

RAINFOREST

CONTENTS

Swamplands

FISHING BIRDS ▼
Different types of fish-eating birds feed on particular types of fish, which reduces competition for food.

The Amazon River in South America carries more water than any other river. Many smaller rivers, called **tributaries**, flow into the Amazon. They add water to it as it flows toward the Atlantic Ocean. Rocks, dirt, twigs, and other materials get carried along too. The river flows more slowly as it nears the ocean. The soil, rocks, and dead plants start falling to the river bottom because the water no longer moves quickly enough to carry them. Fertile soil builds up at the river's **mouth**. It makes the water much shallower, and water plants are able to grow there. When enough soil builds up, it rises above the water's surface in places and becomes home to land animals and plants. This huge patchwork of soil and flowing water creates several distinct **habitats**, each of which is home to a large number of plants and animals. In order to compete for food and space, most plants and animals have developed unique feeding habits, appearances, and behaviors to protect them from **predators**.

▲ SAPROPHYTES
Plants compete for space, especially space in sunlight. Many become suited to growing on the branches of trees. Some are **parasites**. They tap into their **host** and feed from it. Others have hanging roots to take in nutrients. These plants are **saprophytes**. They do not harm the host.

◄ THE ESTUARY
The **estuary** is one of the habitats at the Amazon's mouth. An estuary is the area where a river meets an ocean. The deeper water away from the river banks is home to various species of aquatic animals such as manatees, river dolphins, and caimans. Most estuary animals cannot travel past the point where the river's fresh water meets the ocean's salt water. Some animals are able to move between the ocean and river.

◄ SEED DISPERSAL
Plants must move their seeds to avoid competing for space and light with new plants. Some fish help move seeds. They eat fruits that drop into the water from plants above. They swallow the fruits whole. The seeds pass through the gut of the fish and come out in the droppings. Some find their way to good growing sites.

WETLANDS ►
Many animal species live along the banks of the estuary. The low, flat land is often partly or completely under shallow water. Many fish prefer shallow water, as do turtles and otters. The area attracts many predators, including snakes and other reptiles as well as long-legged birds, which wade into the estuary in search of **prey**.

MARSH LAND ➤

The Amazon floods its banks often, especially during the wet season. Much of the land around the estuary is covered by shallow water at least some of the time. Plants and tree roots provide many hiding places for animals. Water birds often hunt among the tangle of roots, and snapping turtles and small caimans lie in wait for prey. The mud is full of tiny creatures such as worms, snails, and insect larvae.

Bird's-eye view of the edge of the estuary.

FLOODING ➤

Flooding can be good and bad for fish-hunting birds such as the kingfisher. When the water rises, it spreads over a larger area and becomes shallow, allowing the birds to hunt easily. The birds' nests, which are dug into the river banks, are threatened when the water rises too high.

THE FOREST EDGE

The edge of the forest is usually much drier than the swampy wetlands, but it does get flooded. When floods end, the ground remains dotted with pools of still water, which form in hollows. The pools provide an ideal habitat for some amphibians and insects. Much of the dry land is covered by trees and shrubs. Many animals live among the branches of these trees and shrubs because they are safely above the flood line—the highest point flood waters reach. ▼

RAFTS ➤

Various plants float on the surface of the estuary, sending roots down to the river's muddy bottom. They form large rafts which shelter and provide food for all kinds of animals, including manatees.

▼ OLIVACEOUS CORMORANT

This cormorant is named for the olive green sheen of its feathers. Cormorants hunt fish by "flying" underwater. Their feathers absorb water to help them sink. When a cormorant is finished fishing, it must dry its wings before it can fly away.

▲ A jabiru stork inflates its neck like a balloon to warn off enemies or attract a mate.

◄ JABIRU STORK

The jabiru stork is an **opportunistic feeder**, which means it will feed on whatever food is available. It has a bald head and neck, which stay cleaner than feathers when the bird feeds on carrion, or dead, rotting animals.

Swamplands

THE ESTUARY

The Amazon River flows into the Atlantic Ocean. The area where a river meets an ocean is called an **estuary**. Here, the river's fresh water begins to mix with the ocean's salt water. It forms a band of **brackish** water, which is a mix of salt and fresh water. This band is a boundary for most estuary animals, which cannot live in salt water. The boundary moves up and down the river with the rise and fall of the ocean's tides.

MARMOSET ▲

Marmosets are the smallest **primates**. They are hunted by many predators. Marmosets avoid enemies by climbing up to the smallest branches, where many predators cannot follow. The male marmoset above is helping its mate give birth.

▼ SKIMMER

Skimmers are named for the way they feed—by skimming the water's surface with their bills. A skimmer drags the lower half of its bill in the water as it flies above the surface. The top half is smaller, so it stays clear of the water. Skimmers nest on river banks, which frequently flood and drown their young.

A skimmer snaps its bill shut when it feels prey such as fish. ▼

The flamingo sifts by moving its beak up and down and back and forth. ▼

▼ FLAMINGO

Flamingos are the only birds with bills designed to work upside down. A flamingo feeds by taking a mouthful of water and filtering out small **crustaceans** and other animals. It then raises its head to swallow the food.

SCARLET IBIS ▼

Ibises are unspecialized feeders, which means they eat a wide variety of insects, reptiles, amphibians, and other small animals. They nest in groups to provide safety in numbers. When a predator such as a vulture flies above their nests, all the ibises make a noisy fuss to scare it away.

◄ MONK PARAKEETS

These small parrots are noisy, sociable birds. They often make their nests in the tangle of twigs and branches at the bottom of jabiru storks' nests.

SILVER HATCHET FISH

This fish's scales help **camouflage**, or hide it, by reflecting its surroundings. If the fish gets attacked, it can leap from the water and glide for a short distance using its fins like wings. ▼

▼ PIRANHA

There are more than twenty species of piranhas in the Amazon. Most of them are plant-eaters, but the most well-known species, the red-bellied piranha, is a fierce predator. It has razor-sharp teeth that strip an animal's flesh to the bone in seconds. These piranhas attack in schools, but they usually do not attack unless they taste blood.

▲ BANDED KNIFE FISH

This fish can create electricity, which it uses to sense obstacles and food in the murky water. It also stuns its prey and predators with electric shocks.

▲ MANATEE

Manatees are the Amazon's largest **sea mammals**. They are over nine feet (2.75 m) long and weigh over 1000 pounds (450 kg). They breathe at the surface and shut their nostrils under water. Adult manatees eat plants, but babies **nurse**.

▼ UAKARI
Many species of monkeys live in the Amazon area. Uakaris are medium-sized monkeys. They leap among trees or rummage on the ground to find food such as fruit and nuts.

▲ Unlike most monkeys, uakaris are bald and have no facial hair.

WOOD-STORK
Wood-storks build their large nests in trees. The twigs they use can be hard to find. Storks often steal them from one another's nests. When a stork returns to its nest, it brings a stick as a gift for its mate. It then takes over tending the eggs or chicks. ▶

▼ CAIMAN
Caimans are similar to alligators, but they are smaller. They hunt by lying motionless at the water's surface until prey comes near. The caiman sinks under water and strikes from below, pulling its prey down to drown. Large caimans often hunt smaller caimans. Caimans have thick armor-like skin on their bellies, to protect them against attacks from below.

Swamplands

WETLANDS

Wetlands are found around the Amazon estuary. They are areas that are flooded with shallow water most or all of the time. Rafts of water plants are able to grow here by sending roots down into the mud below. The rafts are home to many kinds of animals, and even more animals rely on the rafts for food. Long-legged birds are able to wade in the shallow water in search of food, while smaller animals dive in to catch their prey.

▼ The anaconda squeezes the caiman so tightly that it cannot defend itself or breathe.

◀ ANACONDA
Anacondas are one of the largest snakes in the world. They are up to 30 feet (9 m) in length. They are excellent swimmers that hunt by surprising animals in the water. They coil around their prey and hold it under water until it drowns. The snakes swallow their prey headfirst.

▼ BLACK-BELLIED TREE DUCK
Unlike most ducks, which nest on the ground, black-bellied tree ducks nest in tree trunks. Being off the ground protects the nests and eggs from predators, as well as floods.

◄ NUNBIRD

These birds make their nests in burrows, which they dig into the river banks. The tunnel protects eggs and chicks from large predators. To keep out smaller hunters such as snakes, the birds block the entrance with twigs.

▲ This cross-section shows a nunbird's nest with twigs over the entrance.

◄ The webbed foot of a water opossum acts like a paddle.

WATER OPOSSUM ▼ ►

Many **mammals** have **adapted**, or become suited to, spending time on land as well as in the water. They are called **semiaquatic**. They include otters, water shrews, and water opossums. These animals have slick fur and webbed feet so they swim well.

YELLOW CONURE ▼

This member of the parrot family lives among the wetland trees. Yellow conures nest in holes high up in the trees. Nesting in a hole makes it easier for the birds to defend themselves from enemies, since there is only one way to reach the nest.

▲ The spoon-shaped tip of a spoonbill's round beak.

◄ SPOONBILL

Spoonbills use their flat, unusually shaped bills to sift the mud for prey. The bill's rounded tip has sensors along it which can feel worms and other animals as they move. The birds move their bill from side to side to sift as much mud as possible.

▼ CRESTED CARACARA

Caracaras are small birds of prey. Unlike most birds, they use teamwork to attack and kill larger prey. By ganging up, they can attack and kill larger animals that would be able to defend themselves against just one caracara.

◄ Caracaras attack an egret from two directions at once.

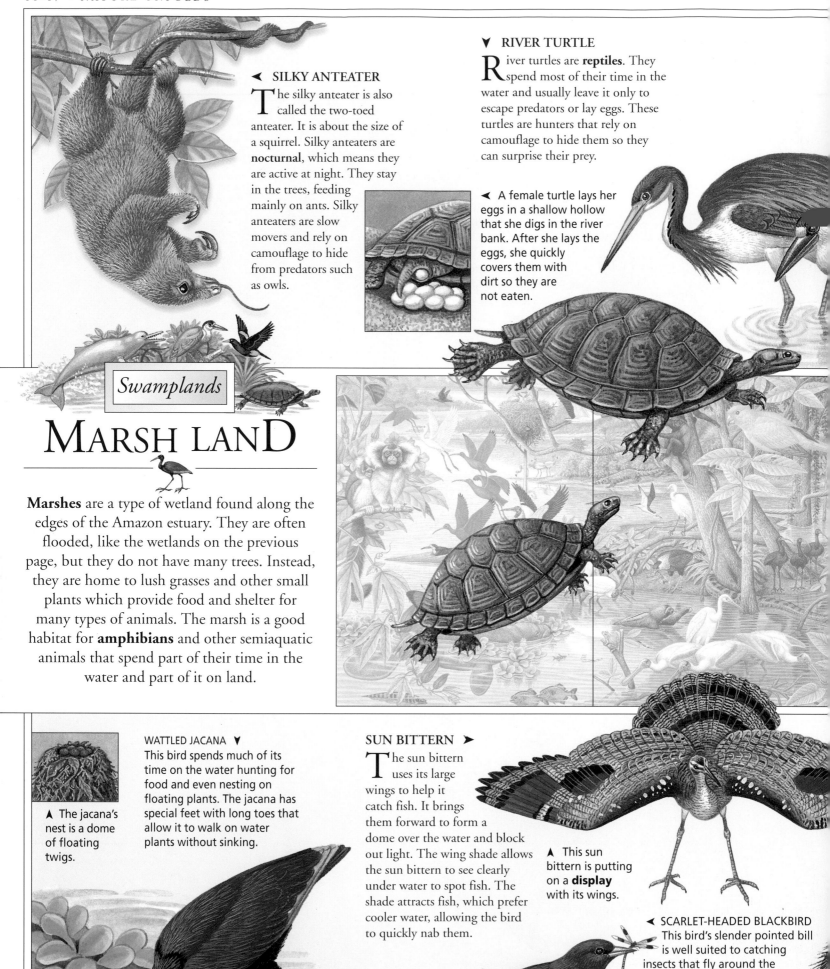

◄ SILKY ANTEATER

The silky anteater is also called the two-toed anteater. It is about the size of a squirrel. Silky anteaters are **nocturnal**, which means they are active at night. They stay in the trees, feeding mainly on ants. Silky anteaters are slow movers and rely on camouflage to hide from predators such as owls.

▼ RIVER TURTLE

River turtles are **reptiles**. They spend most of their time in the water and usually leave it only to escape predators or lay eggs. These turtles are hunters that rely on camouflage to hide them so they can surprise their prey.

◄ A female turtle lays her eggs in a shallow hollow that she digs in the river bank. After she lays the eggs, she quickly covers them with dirt so they are not eaten.

Swamplands

MARSH LAND

Marshes are a type of wetland found along the edges of the Amazon estuary. They are often flooded, like the wetlands on the previous page, but they do not have many trees. Instead, they are home to lush grasses and other small plants which provide food and shelter for many types of animals. The marsh is a good habitat for **amphibians** and other semiaquatic animals that spend part of their time in the water and part of it on land.

WATTLED JACANA ▼

This bird spends much of its time on the water hunting for food and even nesting on floating plants. The jacana has special feet with long toes that allow it to walk on water plants without sinking.

▲ The jacana's nest is a dome of floating twigs.

SUN BITTERN ➤

The sun bittern uses its large wings to help it catch fish. It brings them forward to form a dome over the water and block out light. The wing shade allows the sun bittern to see clearly under water to spot fish. The shade attracts fish, which prefer cooler water, allowing the bird to quickly nab them.

▲ This sun bittern is putting on a **display** with its wings.

◄ SCARLET-HEADED BLACKBIRD

This bird's slender pointed bill is well suited to catching insects that fly around the water's edge and land on reeds and grasses. The bird watches carefully, then plucks them off before they can fly away.

▼ HERONS

Herons are stealthy, slow-moving birds that wade in search of prey such as fish and amphibians. They sneak up on prey and strike so quickly that it does not have time to react and escape. The two shown left are the tricolored, or Louisiana, heron (behind) and the boat-billed heron (in front).

◄ The boat-billed heron feeds on fishes and frogs. It also takes in muddy water with its prey but spits it out before swallowing the food.

▲ HOG-NOSED SKUNK

The hog-nosed skunk is named for its unusual snout, which it uses to sniff out food. It has an excellent sense of smell, so it rarely misses any food that lies in its path.

RIVER DOLPHIN ▼

Unlike most dolphins, river dolphins live in fresh water. When the Amazon floods during the wet season, the river dolphin swims over areas that are usually marshes. It uses a special sense called **echolocation** to detect prey in the murky water.

▲ Rising flood water may drown this calique's chicks.

▼ GOLDEN-WINGED CALIQUE

Caliques use a cunning strategy to protect their eggs and young from predators. They build their nests close to beehives, where snakes and other enemies will not venture. Beehives are often close to the ground, however, and floods are a constant threat in the Amazon. Building their nests near hives protects caliques from one danger but creates another.

◄ BIRD-EATING SPIDER

Bird-eating spiders are among the largest spiders in the world. Some are up to eleven inches (27 cm) across! These spiders jump and pounce on their prey, which includes insects and other **invertebrates**, lizards, and birds. They kill their prey by biting it with their fangs and injecting it with poison.

POTOO ➤

The potoo is a nocturnal bird that relies on camouflage to hide it during the day. Its eyes appear shut, but the potoo can see well enough to spot danger and fly off.

◄ WHITE-FACED SAKI

Male and female saki monkeys have distinct facial markings to help tell individuals apart. The markings also distinguish different species from one another.

◄ The male saki (above) has white fur around its face, and the female (below) has mainly black hair.

◄ KINKAJOU

The kinkajou is a member of the raccoon family. It is well suited to climbing. It has gripping paws and a **prehensile tail**, or one that can wrap around and grip branches. The kinkajou is nocturnal. It eats fruits, eggs, insects, and small animals such as young birds.

The kinkajou explores a termite nest with its tongue. ►

◄ An acrobatic kinkajou plucks a fruit crow out of the air.

Swamplands

FOREST EDGE

Even though the land at the rainforest's edge is not normally under water, it does get flooded occasionally. When a flood ends, pools of water form in holes in the ground. Fish and aquatic animals get left behind in them. The still water is a different habitat from the moving river water, and the fish are hunted by different predators. The forest soil is a mix of **silt** and decayed plant matter, which makes it very fertile.

► A puma catches and kills a young capybara. It kills prey by biting its neck.

PUMA ►

Pumas eat a wide variety of mammals and birds. The capybara is one of the largest animals it hunts in the rainforest. Unlike most large cats, the puma does not roar or growl. It squeals and purrs like a household cat but much more loudly.

▼ CAPYBARA

The capybara is the largest **rodent** in the world. It is semiaquatic and uses its webbed feet to swim. Its head is shaped so that its ears, eyes, and nostrils remain above the water's surface while it swims.

CASTNIID MOTH ►

There are hundreds of species of castniid moths. Most of them are brightly colored. Unlike most moths, which are nocturnal, castniid moths fly during the day. They are often confused with butterflies.

▲ A castniid looking for a mate approaches a hummingbird by mistake.

MARSH DEER ▼

The marsh deer is adapted to grazing on reeds and other plants that grow in its wet habitat. It has long, sleek legs to keep its body away from the water and mud. Its large hoofs prevent it from sinking into the mud.

▲ A cacao pod cut open to show the beans inside (left). Pods growing on the tree trunk (above). The cacao flower (right).

◄ CACAO

Like most rainforest trees, the cacao is an **evergreen**, which means it does not shed its leaves. The cacao tree grows up to 40 feet (12 m) high. Its seeds, or beans, are used for making cocoa. They grow in pods, which are the tree's fruit.

HOATZIN ➤

The hoatzin is nicknamed the "reptile bird." Adult hoatzins are weak swimmers, but their babies are not. When an enemy approaches, the chicks drop from the nest to the water below and swim until it leaves. They climb back to the nest using the claws they have on each wing.

▲ Baby hoatzins have wing claws, but adults do not.

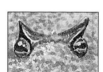

Baby hoatzin swimming ➤

▼ GIANT RIVER OTTER

River otters are well suited to swimming. They have a streamlined body, webbed feet, and a flattened tail. The tail helps push the otter through the water and it also acts as a rudder for steering.

▲ The kingfisher moves and steers under water with its wings. When it catches a fish with its sharp bill, the bird returns to its perch to eat it.

▲ AMAZON KINGFISHER

The forest edge is an ideal habitat for kingfishers, especially when flood waters create small pools. The birds perch above the pools. When they spot a fish, they plunge into the water headfirst to seize their prey.

GIANT HORNED FROG ▼

This frog is named for the folds of skin over its eyes. It uses its camouflage to blend in with its surroundings and then waits for prey to come near. It eats mice, rats, large insects, and other frogs.

▲ The frog buries itself in the sand to escape predators.

Kinkajou (53)

Swamplands

KEY TO FOLD-OUT

White-Faced Saki (52)

Use these key numbers if you want to identify the animals and plants on the Swamplands fold-out. Most of them are featured on pages 12-19, and they are listed here in bold type. Animals that are not featured are also keyed and listed here with a brief description.

8 **Banded Knife Fish**
9 **Piranha**
10 Water Hyacinth
   This water plant is an important source of food for Amazon manatees. (see 12).
11 **Silver Hatchet Fish**
12 **Manatee**
13 Jaguar (see page 34)
14 **Wood-Stork**
15 **Flamingo**
16 **Monk Parakeet**

1 **Olivaceous Cormorant**
2 **Scarlet Ibis**
3 Great Ibis
   This bird is at home in swampy areas. It has long legs for wading in shallow water. Its long, curved beak is ideal for catching fish and frogs.
4 **Marmoset**
5 **Skimmer**
6 Agrias
   The shades of this butterfly's wings change depending on the light.
7 Passiflora
   This vine is common in the rainforest.

17 **Jabiru Stork and chicks**
18 **Black-Faced Uakari**
19 **Caiman**
20 Cattle Egret
   This small heron feeds on small fish and amphibians.
21 **Crested Caracara**
22 **Three-Toed Sloth** (see page 32)

Bird-Eating Spider (43)

Skimmer (5)

23 Vaillant's Frog
Like other frogs that live in tropical areas, Vaillant's frog thrives in the wet swamplands habitat. It needs to breed in water and the humid air keeps its skin moist.

24 Mud Turtle
This reptile hides in the muddy edges of the swamp, waiting for prey to pass by.

25 **Spoonbill**

26 Great Egret
This bird feeds on fish and amphibians.

27 **Anaconda**

33 Cryptic Katydid
This winged insect is camouflaged to look like a leaf, which helps it hide from predators.

34 **Scarlet-Headed Blackbird**

35 **River Turtle**

36 **Boat-Billed Heron**

37 **River Dolphin**

38 **Tricolored Heron**

39 **Hog-Nosed Skunk**

40 **Silky Anteater**

41 White Ibis.
This ibis is similar to its cousin, the green ibis, but its feathers are a different color.

42 **Golden-Winged Calique**

43 **Bird-Eating Spider**

44 **Sun Bittern**

45 **Capybara**

46 **Wattled Jacana**

47 Pierid Butterfly
The pierid butterflies are a huge group and are found all over the world.

48 **Giant River Otter**

Yellow Conures (29)

River Turtle (35)

28 Green Ibis
Different species of ibises have distinctively colored feathers to avoid confusion during the mating season. The green ibis is named for the sheen of its feathers.

29 **Yellow Conure**

30 **Nunbird**

31 **Water Opossum**

32 **Black-Bellied Tree Duck**

49 **Giant Horned Frog**

50 **Marsh Deer**

51 **Potoo**

52 **White-Faced Saki**

53 **Kinkajou**

54 **Hoatzin and chicks**

55 **Puma**

56 **Cacao**

57 **Amazon Kingfisher**

58 **Castniid Moth**

59 Juanulloa
The juanulloa is a relative of the potato. It grows both on trees and on the ground.

Manatees (12)

Marmosets (4)

Rainforest

Rainforests are named for the large amounts of rain that fall on them every year—at least 80 inches (200 cm). It rains almost every day in rainforests. The Amazon rainforest is very lush. The trees are so thick that sunlight does not reach the ground. This forest is home to more types of animals than any other place on Earth. To make the rainforest easier to study, scientists divide it into four main layers: the forest floor, the understory, the lower canopy, and the upper canopy. Each layer is home to different animals.

UPPER CANOPY ▶

The canopy is a dense layer formed by the trees' highest branches. The branches are so thick that they form a "roof" over the forest below and block out much of the sunlight. Many flowers and fruits grow here, where they get plenty of light. They provide food for all kinds of animals, from insects to birds and monkeys.

◀ LIANAS

Some rainforest plants rely on others to hold them up. **Lianas** attach themselves to young trees and eventually wind their way up to the sunny canopy.

LOWER CANOPY ▶

The branches are sturdier at this level than in the upper canopy. Larger animals such as monkeys and sloths climb and rest on them. The animals are so well suited to moving among the branches that many never touch the ground. They simply leap, swing, and fly from tree to tree.

▶ DISPERSAL

Rainforest plants must spread their seeds so they will find enough room and light to grow. One of the best ways to move seeds is through animals. Plants produce fruit that contain seeds. Animals eat the fruit and the seeds. The seeds are dispersed in the animals' droppings.

POLLINATION ▼

Flowers must be **pollinated** before they can make seeds. Most flowers have bright colors, strong scents, and sweet nectar to attract birds and other animals. As the animals eat the nectar, they get covered in pollen, which may rub off on the next flower they visit.

FOREST FLOOR ▲

It is very dark along the ground of the rainforest. The leaves above are so thick that almost no sunlight reaches the ground, and few small plants are able to grow here. The ground is covered with rotting fruit, branches, and leaves that fall from the trees above. Spiders, insects, lizards, toads, and small mammals roam around the forest floor. The largest predators are jaguars and poisonous snakes.

UNDERSTORY ▲

The understory is the layer of forest between the leafy canopy and the dark forest floor. Small trees, shrubs, and palms are found here. Few animals live in this part of the forest, but many climb, swing, and fly through it. Birds often nest here to hide from larger hunting birds, which rest in the canopy above.

DECOMPOSITION ▼

When plants and animals die in the rainforest, they are quickly broken down by **decomposers** such as worms, bacteria, and these fungi.

GERMINATION

When seeds land in a good spot, they may begin to grow, or **germinate**. Some get a little extra help. Seeds that pass through animals are surrounded by dung, which is an ideal fertilizer. Many trees make seeds with a lot of stored food. The food allows the seeds to grow into young trees without sunlight. ▶

Tropic of Cancer

The Equator

Tropic of Capricorn

▨ Tropical rainforest

Rainforest

UPPER CANOPY

The upper canopy gets the most sunlight. The plants grow so thickly that the canopy forms a solid layer of greenery, allowing little light to filter through. Many **epiphytes** are found here. Epiphytes are plants that grow on the branches of trees, where they can reach the sunlight. Most have dangling roots to pull water from the air, but some dig into their host and feed on it.

WHITE-COLLARED SWIFT ►

Insects are an important source of food for many animals in the rainforest. Swifts spend most of their time in the air catching flying insects. They are small birds, but their long, strong wings allow them to stay in flight for several hours at a time.

KING VULTURE ►

Animals cannot see far amid the thick leaves of the canopy. The king vulture relies on its excellent sense of smell to find the dead animals on which it feeds.

▲ The king vulture has a wing span of six feet (nearly 2 m).

SQUIRREL MONKEY ►

Squirrel monkeys are small and light enough to move easily in the canopy. They can reach fruits without breaking thin branches or falling. They also leap easily from the small branches of one tree to those of another.

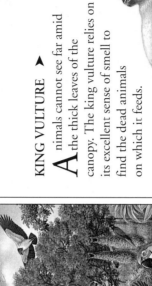

SWALLOWTAIL KITE ►

Catching prey can be difficult among the dense leaves of the canopy. The swallowtail kite goes after small birds in midair, before they have a chance to escape.

► **RED-RUFFED FRUIT CROW**

Many animals have become **specialized feeders.** For example, some eat only seeds or berries. Since berries grow year-round on different trees, birds such as the fruit crow can always find something to eat.

A harpy eagle snatches a small monkey from the trees. ►

CAPUCHIN MONKEY ▶

Capuchins are heavier than squirrel monkeys, but they are still light enough to move among the branches of the upper canopy. They eat fruit, nuts, and leaves. Capuchins also hunt for insects and small animals such as birds and lizards. Sometimes they move to lower levels to play and search for food.

▲ Capuchin monkeys raid birds' nests for eggs.

▼ OROPENDOLA

It can be difficult finding a nesting place that is safe from enemies. The oropendola solves this problem by building a hanging nest. It uses its beak to weave together pieces of plants such as grass stems and strips of leaves. The woven nest is very strong. Since it hangs, it is difficult for most predators to reach. The female builds the nest while the male performs a mating **display**.

▼ MORPHO BUTTERFLY

Male morphos have vivid blue wings, which helps them attract females. Females are dull brown. Females pick the largest and bluest male to be their mate.

▼ BLACK-THROATED TROGON

Trogons are well suited to clinging to tree trunks. Two of the four toes on each foot point backward, which allows the bird to grip bark. Stiff tail feathers help support the bird while it clings to the trunk and pecks in search of small insects.

▼ Macaws live in very cramped quarters.

◀ HARPY EAGLE

The harpy eagle is the largest bird in the rainforest. It has fairly short wings for darting between branches after such prey as monkeys, sloths, and other small mammals.

MACAWS ◀

These colorful long-tailed parrots often nibble on soft rocks. Their food does not contain all of the **nutrients** they need, and the rocks provide important minerals. Their nests are made in small tree hollows. The parents have to clamber over their chicks to feed them. Things get very cramped by the time the chicks are ready to leave the nest.

▲ A chick begins to resemble its parents when its feathers grow in.

Rainforest

LOWER CANOPY

This layer is the busiest one in the tropical forest. The branches here are thicker than in the upper canopy, so they can hold larger, heavier animals.

Since the upper canopy blocks a lot of the sunlight, the lower canopy is much darker. The animals cannot always see well in the dim light. Most rely on other senses to find their way around, locate food, and avoid danger.

▲ ORCHID BEE
Orchid bees pollinate orchids as they collect pollen and nectar to eat.

HOWLER MONKEYS ►

Large monkeys such as the howlers are too heavy to climb above the branches of the lower canopy. They often lose sight of each other in the dim lower canopy, so they rely on their voices to communicate. Their loud, booming howl is created by forcing air through their extra-large voice box.

◄ The air-sac in the howler's throat inflates to force air through the voice box, or larynx.

GREEN-CHEEKED HUMMINGBIRD ►

Hummingbirds are the smallest birds. They are so tiny that they can build their nests on the thinnest twigs and leaves. They are able to hover like helicopters, which allows them to hang in the air and suck nectar from dangling flowers.

Birds and lizards often check bromeliads for the prey shown here. ►

◄ QUETZAL
While hovering under the branches, this rare bird feeds by grabbing insects and fruit from trees .

TOUCANS ►

Most people can recognize toucans by their large, colorful beaks. The birds use their beaks to signal to each other across the forest canopy. Their long, lightweight bill also allows toucans to reach and pick fruits off branches that are too thin to support their body weight.

Toucans toss fruit into the air to pass it from their beak to their throat. ►

▲ An ancient Olmec carving of a quetzal.

SPIDER MONKEYS

Spider monkeys have a **prehensile tail**, which means they can use it to grab branches as if it were an extra arm. It has a leathery pad that provides better grip. These lightweight monkeys can reach most fruits by hanging from their tail. They also use their tails to escape predators by swinging quickly from branch to branch. ►

► The pad is on the underside of the tail.

▲ EMERALD TREE BOA

The emerald tree boa is well camouflaged among leafy branches, and it can strike quickly to surprise its prey. Boas kill their prey by squeezing it until it can no longer breathe. They swallow prey whole, and a single meal may last them several days.

A woodpecker drilling holes ▶

▼ WOODPECKER

The woodpecker feeds mainly on grubs. It taps bark with its beak to feel and listen for the hollows grubs live in. When it finds a grub, it hammers a hole with its beak and grabs the prey. Woodpeckers have special skulls that absorb the shock of hammering.

▼ The woodpecker coils its long tongue inside its skull when not using it.

BRAZIL NUT ▶

These nuts are similar in shape to an orange segment and grow inside a large, round fruit. When the fruit falls from a branch, it hits other branches on its way to the forest floor. It bursts and scatters the nuts, which are large seeds.

▼ Brazil nut

BROMELIADS ▲

These plants are **epiphytes.** They grow on the branches of trees but do not harm them. Their hanging roots collect water from the air. Bromeliads also collect rainwater in their funnel-shaped leaves. The pools of water in their leaves provide a home to various small animals, such as tree frogs, snails, and leeches.

GECKO ▲ Geckos have special feet that can grip even the most slippery leaves.

▼ TWO-TOED SLOTH

Two-toed sloths are smaller and more active than their cousin, the three-toed sloth. Sloths are the slowest moving land animals. Since they cannot outrun enemies, sloths avoid being eaten by gripping branches so tightly that they cannot be pulled down.

◀ The sloth skull shows the cheek teeth, which the animal uses to chew its food.

▲ Each front limb has two toes.

MOUSE OPOSSUM

Opossums are the only group of **marsupials** found outside of Australia. Baby marsupials are tiny when they are born. They move to a pouch on their mother's body, where they keep growing. When they are big enough to leave the pouch, they ride on their mother's back. ▶

▲ CATTLEYA ORCHID This orchid is an epiphyte.

▼ RHINOCEROS BEETLE

Adult males have a growth like a rhinoceros horn, which is how they got their name. They use the horn to fight with other males. The winner gets to mate with the female of his choice. These beetles can be up to five inches (13 cm) long.

Rainforest
UNDERSTORY

The understory is a dark place. Few animals spend all their time here. It is crisscrossed mainly by animals on their way to the canopy or the forest floor. Some birds and mammals nest and raise their young in the smaller trees, where they can hide from many of the large hunting birds that fly above the canopy. Many other predators hunt in the understory so the young must be guarded closely.

LEAF-CUTTER ANT
These ants have scissor-like jaws for cutting leaves. They carry the pieces to their nests and leave them to grow mold, which they eat.

TREE PORCUPINE
This porcupine has shorter quills than ground-living ones because it must be able to climb between branches easily. To rest, the porcupine wraps its tail around a branch and hangs upside-down. It feeds mainly on leaves.

SPECTACLED OWL
The spectacled owl is an excellent nocturnal hunter. With sharp eyesight and silent wings, it swoops down and snatches animals by surprise.

FRUIT BAT
Fruit bats have a long snout that allows them to smell food from a distance. Their large eyes and ears enable them to see and hear clearly while they fly among the trees at night.

RUBY TOPAZ HUMMINGBIRD
Hummingbirds flap their wings so quickly that they appear to be a blur. The wings move back and forth, holding the bird still while it feeds on the nectar of a flower.

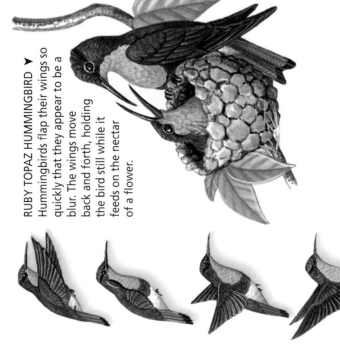

These pictures show how its wings move when a hummingbird hovers.

THREE-TOED SLOTH
This sloth has a type of algae growing on its fur. The algae turn from green to brown at different times of the year and help camouflage the sloth. Sloths have such weak legs that they cannot walk. They hang from branches and rarely go down to the ground.

Moths feed on the algae that grow on sloths.

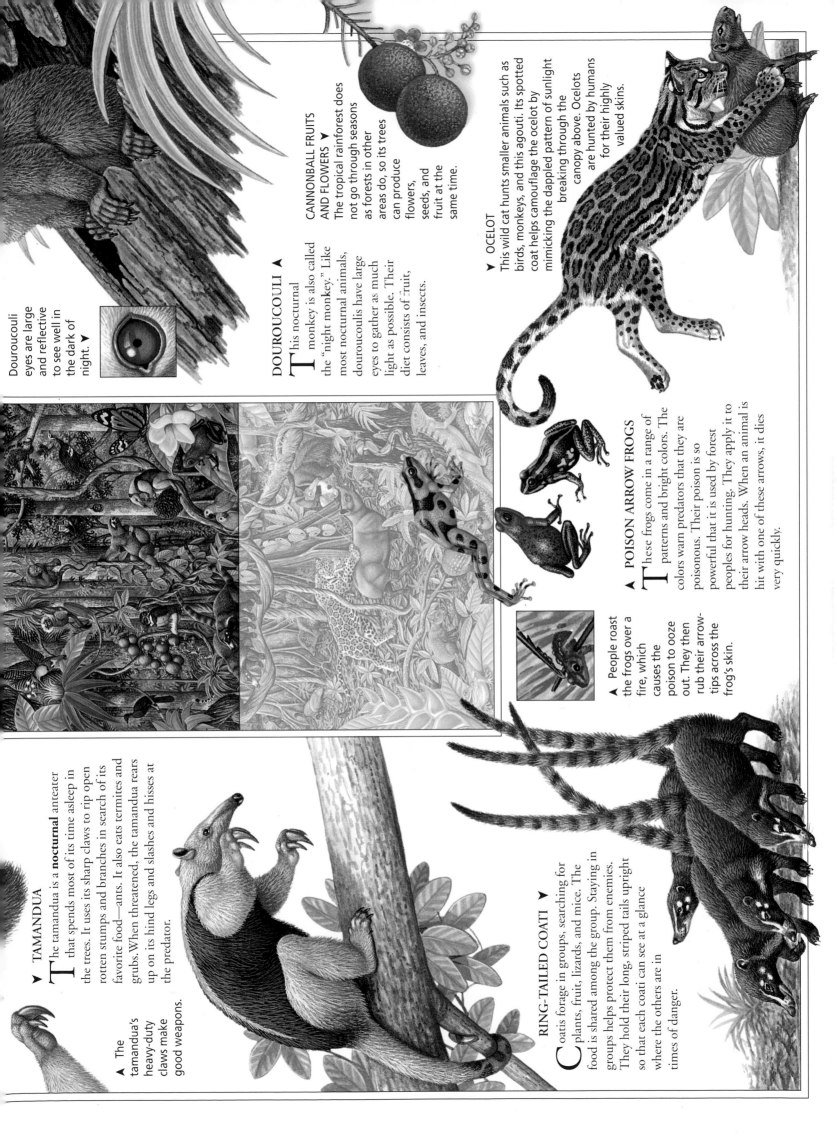

Douroucouli eyes are large and reflective to see well in the dark of night. ▶

DOUROUCOULI ▲

This nocturnal monkey is also called the "night monkey." Like most nocturnal animals, douroucoulis have large eyes to gather as much light as possible. Their diet consists of fruit, leaves, and insects.

CANNONBALL FRUITS AND FLOWERS

The tropical rainforest does not go through seasons as forests in other areas do, so its trees can produce flowers, seeds, and fruit at the same time.

▼ OCELOT

This wild cat hunts smaller animals such as birds, monkeys, and this agouti. Its spotted coat helps camouflage the ocelot by mimicking the dappled pattern of sunlight breaking through the canopy above. Ocelots are hunted by humans for their highly valued skins.

▲ POISON ARROW FROGS

These frogs come in a range of patterns and bright colors. The colors warn predators that they are poisonous. Their poison is so powerful that it is used by forest peoples for hunting. They apply it to their arrow heads. When an animal is hit with one of these arrows, it dies very quickly.

▲ People roast the frogs over a fire, which causes the poison to ooze out. They then rub their arrow-tips across the frog's skin.

▶ TAMANDUA

The tamandua is a **nocturnal** anteater that spends most of its time asleep in the trees. It uses its sharp claws to rip open rotten stumps and branches in search of its favorite food—ants. It also eats termites and grubs. When threatened, the tamandua rears up on its hind legs and slashes and hisses at the predator.

▲ The tamandua's heavy-duty claws make good weapons.

RING-TAILED COATI ▶

Coatis forage in groups, searching for plants, fruit, lizards, and mice. The food is shared among the group. Staying in groups helps protect them from enemies. They hold their long, striped tails upright so that each coati can see at a glance where the others are in times of danger.

Rainforest

FOREST FLOOR

When fruits, leaves, branches, and even dead animals fall from the higher layers of the rainforest, they usually end up on the forest floor. Fungi, bacteria, and **invertebrates** feed on and break down the decaying plants and animals. They help create a thin layer of fertile soil called **humus**. Besides small, ground-living animals, the largest animals of the Amazon are also found on the forest floor.

► BROCKET DEER
This deer is well suited to the dense forest. It is small enough to slip easily between shrubs and other plants. Its antlers point backward, so they do not snag on branches when it runs from enemies.

JAGUAR ►
These big cats are usually tan with darker spots, but sometimes they are black. Jaguars like the water and are usually found near streams or rivers. They are active at night, when they hunt large land animals such as deer, capybaras, and tapirs. Jaguars quietly creep up on their prey and then leap on it by surprise. They bite the animal's neck with their powerful jaws. Jaguars also hunt other prey, such as fish. They sit patiently on fallen logs and snatch the fish out of the water with their sharp claws.

► TAYRA
The tayra is related to weasels, otters, badgers, and skunks. Tayras are good swimmers and climbers. They eat a wide variety of foods, including fruit and small animals such as squirrels and birds. In turn, they are hunted by jaguars. Tayras are often found in pairs or family groups.

► The tayra is a good hunter on the ground and in the trees.

► Tayras often raid nests to snatch eggs or chicks.

► Its front claws are so big that an anteater must walk on its knuckles.

▶ BOA CONSTRICTOR

Boa constrictors ambush their prey. They quickly coil around the surprised animal and squeeze, or constrict, it so that it cannot breathe. When the animal dies, the snake dislocates, or unhinges, its jaws and swallows its prey headfirst.

ARMADILLO ▶

Armadillos are protected from the teeth and claws of predators by bony plates of armor. They have powerful claws on their front feet, which they use to dig for insects. They are active mainly at night, when they also hunt for small reptiles and amphibians.

▶ The tapir's snout is soft and flexible.

TAPIR

Tapirs have a sensitive snout, which they use to sniff out fallen fruits and nuts on the forest floor. Baby tapirs have a pattern of stripes and spots that helps camouflage them on the dappled ground. ▶

▶ BASILISK LIZARD

This unusual lizard can walk on water. It moves so quickly over the surface that its feet touch the water for only a split-second, so it does not have time to sink. The basilisk dashes across water only when it is in danger.

GIANT ANTEATER ▲

◀ Anteater skull

▲ An anteater can flick its tongue more than 100 times a minute when feeding.

Giant anteaters have very strong front legs with huge claws. They use them to rip open termite and ant nests. They use their long, sticky tongue to lap up thousands of insects. Anteaters have a tube-shaped mouth with no teeth. Baby anteaters ride on their mother's back until they are big enough to fend for themselves.

▶ COLLARED PECCARY

Peccaries are wild hogs. They forage in large herds and can be dangerous. Other animals often flee from peccary herds because peccaries will attack from all sides. They eat almost anything.

▶ A peccary has sharp teeth to rip flesh and flat ones to grind plants.

TRUMPETER BIRD ▶

These birds are named for their trumpet-like call. They work together to hunt snakes. One bird pecks the snake's head while the others hold it.

Rainforest

KEY TO FOLD-OUT

Use these key numbers if you want to identify any of the animals and plants on the Rainforest fold-out. Most of them are featured on pages 28-35, and they are listed here in bold type. Animals that are not featured are keyed, listed, and described here.

1 **Swallow-Tailed Kite**
2 **Yellow-Chevroned Parakeet**
  Parakeets are small parrots with long tails. They eat fruit, seeds, and nuts.
3 **Harpy Eagle**
4 **White-Collared Swift**
5 **Black-Throated Trogon**
6 Tanager
  Tanagers eat fruit, seeds, and a few insects. Some species are among the most colorful birds in the world.
7 **Yellow Conure** (see page 15)
8 **Red-Ruffed Fruit Crow**
9 **King Vulture**
10 **Oropendola**
11 **Squirrel Monkey**

White-Collared
Swifts (4)

39 Tamarin
  Tamarins are miniature monkeys. They feed on fruit, eggs, and insects.
40 **Ruby Topaz Hummingbird**
41 **Passion Flower**
  The passion flower is a climbing vine. Its flowers are waxy and tough enough to survive the beaks of hummingbirds.
42 Guan
  These birds of the forest floor are drawn to fire. Native peoples hunt them by using flaming torches as lures.
43 **Cannonball Fruits and Flowers**
44 **Ocelot**
45 **Spectacled Owl**
46 **Three-Toed Sloth**
47 **Douroucouli**
48 Rufous Jacamar
  Jacamars are similar to hummingbirds, but they eat insects instead of nectar.
49 Ithomiid Butterfly
  There are many species of these colorful butterflies in the Amazon rainforest. They gather in groups to feed on forest flowers.
50 **Tamandua**
51 **Leaf-Cutter Ant**
52 **Brocket Deer**
53 **Ring-Tailed Coati**
54 **Tayra**
55 **Trumpeter Bird**
56 **Collared Peccary**
57 **Giant Anteater**
58 **Boa Constrictor**
59 **Armadillo**
60 **Tapir**
61 **Jaguar**
62 Lobster Claw
  The clusters of this plant are designed to attract pollinating animals.

Quetzal (22)

Woodpecker (21)

Three-Toed
Sloth (46)

12 Three-Wattle Bellbird
These birds belong to a family of birds
that are known as "chatterers," because
they are so noisy.

13 Capuchin Monkey
14 Macaw
15 Morpho Butterfly
16 Toucan
17 Green Aracari
This small bird is related to toucans.

18 Parrot
Parrots are smaller than macaws and
have short, squared tails. Their strong
beaks allow them to eat many kinds of
fruit and seeds, and they use their feet
to hold their food.

19 Spider Monkey
20 Howler Monkey
21 Woodpecker
22 Quetzal
23 Emerald Tree Boa
24 Woolly Monkey
These monkeys are named for their
woolly fur. Their hands and feet are
bare, so they can climb well.

25 Two-Toed Sloth
26 Rhinoceros Beetle
27 Mouse Opossum
28 Bromeliad
29 Poison Arrow Frog
30 Green-Cheeked
    Hummingbird
31 Cattleya Orchid
32 Brazil Nut
33 Orchid Bee
34 Gecko
35 Tree Porcupine
36 Motmot
These birds perch in trees
and use their beaks to snatch
insects as they fly by. They
also eat snails, lizards, and fruit.

37 Fruit Bat
38 Red-Faced Uakari (see page14)

Emerald Tree Boa (23)

Jaguar (61)

63 Red-Eyed Tree Frog
When this frog crouches flat on a leaf
and closes its colorful eyes, it is very
well camouflaged.

64 Agouti
The agouti is a rodent. Its fur and
meat are valued by the forest peoples
of Brazil.

65 Paca
The pale markings on the paca's
coat camouflage it from predators by
mimicking the dappled sunlight on
the dark forest floor.

66 Acuchi
This rodent is closely related to the
agouti. It is known for its habit of
storing food, which is an unusual
behavior in the rainforest, since food
is available year-round.

67 **Basilisk Lizard**
68 Golden Beetle
This beetle is just one of the hundreds
of species that live in the tropical
forest. Its metallic, mirror-like sheen
may confuse enemies.

Poison Arrow
Frogs (29)

NATURE UNFOLDS

THE TROPICAL RAINFOREST

—— G L O S S A R Y ——

adapted Describes a plant or animal that has become well suited to its environment

amphibians A group of animals, including frogs and toads, that begin their life in the water and move to land when they become adults

brackish Describes a mixture of fresh and salt water

camouflage Patterns or colors that help an animal blend in with its surroundings

crustacean A group of sea animals including shrimp and lobsters, which have their skeleton on the outside of their body and have several pairs of legs

decomposer An organism such as fungus, that breaks down dead plant or animal matter, and makes nutrients for the environment

display A dance or other behavior performed by an animal to attract attention or warn off danger

echolocation An animal's ability to locate objects by sending out and receiving sound waves

epiphyte A plant that makes its own food and "piggybacks" on another plant

estuary The part of a river that meets the ocean, where fresh and salt water mix

evergreen A tree or plant that remains green all year

germinate To cause to sprout or grow

habitat The natural place where a plant or animal is found

humus A type of soil that is created from decayed plants and animals

host An animal or plant on which another organism lives

invertebrate Describes animals such as worms and insects, which do not have a backbone

liana A climbing plant with long, ropelike stems

mammal A group of warm-blooded animals whose bodies are covered with hair or fur. Female mammals are the only animals that make milk in their body to feed their young.

marsh A type of wetland which is always or almost always covered in water and which does not have many trees

marsupial Mammals that have a pouch to carry their young

mouth The part of a river or stream where it meets another body of water

nocturnal Describes an animal that is active at night

nurse To suckle milk from a mother's body

nutrient A substance that animals and plants need in order to stay healthy and strong

Olmec An ancient group of native people who lived in what is now southern Mexico

opportunistic feeder An animal that feeds on a wide variety of animals and plants, depending on what is available

parasite A plant or animal that attaches itself to another creature and feeds off of it

pollination The movement of dustlike particles of pollen from the flower of one plant to the flower of another; after being pollinated, a flower can make seeds

predator An animal that hunts and kills the animals it eats

prey An animal that is hunted and eaten by other animals

primate Mammals that include people, apes, and monkeys, and whose members have special hands instead of paws

rainforest A forest that receives at least 80 inches (203 cm) of rain each year, and which has trees at least 98 feet (30 m) tall; tropical rainforests are at least 75°F (24°C) year-round

reptile A group of cold-blooded animals that have backbones and whose leathery skin is covered with scales

rodent Mammals with large, sharp front teeth that never stop growing

saprophyte An organism that grows on and gets its nourishment from dead or decaying organic matter

semiaquatic Describes an animal that spends part of its time on land and part of its time in the water, usually to hunt

specialized feeder An animal that feeds only on specific types of plants or animals

silt A type of soil made up of dirt and finely ground rock, which is carried by rivers and then deposited when the water begins to slow down

tributary A stream that flows into a larger stream or body of water